2017 SQA Past Papers with Answers

Higher
COMPUTING SCIENCE

2015, 2016 & 2017 Exams

HODDER GIBSON
AN HACHETTE UK COMPANY

This book contains the official SQA 2015, 2016 and 2017 Exams for Higher Computing Science, with associated SQA-approved answers modified from the official marking instructions that accompany the paper.

In addition the book contains study skills advice. This advice has been specially commissioned by Hodder Gibson, and has been written by experienced senior teachers and examiners in line with the Higher for CfE syllabus and assessment outlines. This is not SQA material but has been devised to provide further guidance for Higher examinations.

Hodder Gibson is grateful to the copyright holders, as credited on the final page of the Answer section, for permission to use their material. Every effort has been made to trace the copyright holders and to obtain their permission for the use of copyright material. Hodder Gibson will be happy to receive information allowing us to rectify any error or omission in future editions.

Hachette UK's policy is to use papers that are natural, renewable and recyclable products and made from wood grown in sustainable forests. The logging and manufacturing processes are expected to conform to the environmental regulations of the country of origin.

Orders: please contact Bookpoint Ltd, 130 Park Drive, Milton Park, Abingdon, Oxon OX14 4SE. Telephone: (44) 01235 827720. Fax: (44) 01235 400454. Lines are open 9.00–5.00, Monday to Saturday, with a 24-hour message answering service. Visit our website at www.hoddereducation.co.uk. Hodder Gibson can be contacted direct on: Tel: 0141 333 4650; Fax: 0141 404 8188; email: hoddergibson@hodder.co.uk

This collection first published in 2017 by
Hodder Gibson, an imprint of Hodder Education,
An Hachette UK Company
211 St Vincent Street
Glasgow G2 5QY

Typeset by Aptara, Inc.

Printed in the UK

A catalogue record for this title is available from the British Library

ISBN: 978-1-5104-2145-5

2 1

2018 2017

MIX
Paper from
responsible sources
FSC™ C104740

Introduction

Study Skills – what you need to know to pass exams!

Pause for thought

Many students might skip quickly through a page like this. After all, we all know how to revise. Do you really though?

Think about this:

"IF YOU ALWAYS DO WHAT YOU ALWAYS DO, YOU WILL ALWAYS GET WHAT YOU HAVE ALWAYS GOT."

Do you like the grades you get? Do you want to do better? If you get full marks in your assessment, then that's great! Change nothing! This section is just to help you get that little bit better than you already are.

There are two main parts to the advice on offer here. The first part highlights fairly obvious things but which are also very important. The second part makes suggestions about revision that you might not have thought about but which WILL help you.

Part 1

DOH! It's so obvious but …

Start revising in good time

Don't leave it until the last minute – this will make you panic.

Make a revision timetable that sets out work time AND play time.

Sleep and eat!

Obvious really, and very helpful. Avoid arguments or stressful things too – even games that wind you up. You need to be fit, awake and focused!

Know your place!

Make sure you know exactly **WHEN and WHERE** your exams are.

Know your enemy!

Make sure you know what to expect in the exam.

How is the paper structured?

How much time is there for each question?

What types of question are involved?

Which topics seem to come up time and time again?

Which topics are your strongest and which are your weakest?

Are all topics compulsory or are there choices?

Learn by DOING!

There is no substitute for past papers and practice papers – they are simply essential! Tackling this collection of papers and answers is exactly the right thing to be doing as your exams approach.

Part 2

People learn in different ways. Some like low light, some bright. Some like early morning, some like evening / night. Some prefer warm, some prefer cold. But everyone uses their BRAIN and the brain works when it is active. Passive learning – sitting gazing at notes – is the most INEFFICIENT way to learn anything. Below you will find tips and ideas for making your revision more effective and maybe even more enjoyable. What follows gets your brain active, and active learning works!

Activity 1 – Stop and review

Step 1

When you have done no more than 5 minutes of revision reading STOP!

Step 2

Write a heading in your own words which sums up the topic you have been revising.

Step 3

Write a summary of what you have revised in no more than two sentences. Don't fool yourself by saying, "I know it, but I cannot put it into words". That just means you don't know it well enough. If you cannot write your summary, revise that section again, knowing that you must write a summary at the end of it. Many of you will have notebooks full of blue/black ink writing. Many of the pages will not be especially attractive or memorable so try to liven them up a bit with colour as you are reviewing and rewriting. **This is a great memory aid, and memory is the most important thing.**

Activity 2 – Use technology!

Why should everything be written down? Have you thought about "mental" maps, diagrams, cartoons and colour to help you learn? And rather than write down notes, why not record your revision material?

What about having a text message revision session with friends? Keep in touch with them to find out how and what they are revising and share ideas and questions.

Why not make a video diary where you tell the camera what you are doing, what you think you have learned and what you still have to do? No one has to see or hear it, but the process of having to organise your thoughts in a formal way to explain something is a very important learning practice.

Be sure to make use of electronic files. You could begin to summarise your class notes. Your typing might be slow, but it will get faster and the typed notes will be easier to read than the scribbles in your class notes. Try to add different fonts and colours to make your work stand out. You can easily Google relevant pictures, cartoons and diagrams which you can copy and paste to make your work more attractive and **MEMORABLE**.

Activity 3 – This is it. Do this and you will know lots!

Step 1

In this task you must be very honest with yourself! Find the SQA syllabus for your subject (www.sqa.org.uk). Look at how it is broken down into main topics called MANDATORY knowledge. That means stuff you MUST know.

Step 2

BEFORE you do ANY revision on this topic, write a list of everything that you already know about the subject. It might be quite a long list but you only need to write it once. It shows you all the information that is already in your long-term memory so you know what parts you do not need to revise!

Step 3

Pick a chapter or section from your book or revision notes. Choose a fairly large section or a whole chapter to get the most out of this activity.

With a buddy, use Skype, Facetime, Twitter or any other communication you have, to play the game "If this is the answer, what is the question?". For example, if you are revising Geography and the answer you provide is "meander", your buddy would have to make up a question like "What is the word that describes a feature of a river where it flows slowly and bends often from side to side?".

Make up 10 "answers" based on the content of the chapter or section you are using. Give this to your buddy to solve while you solve theirs.

Step 4

Construct a wordsearch of at least 10 × 10 squares. You can make it as big as you like but keep it realistic. Work together with a group of friends. Many apps allow you to make wordsearch puzzles online. The words and phrases can go in any direction and phrases can be split. Your puzzle must only contain facts linked to the topic you are revising. Your task is to find 10 bits of information to hide in your puzzle, but you must not repeat information that you used in Step 3. DO NOT show where the words are. Fill up empty squares with random letters. Remember to keep a note of where your answers are hidden but do not show your friends. When you have a complete puzzle, exchange it with a friend to solve each other's puzzle.

Step 5

Now make up 10 questions (not "answers" this time) based on the same chapter used in the previous two tasks. Again, you must find NEW information that you have not yet used. Now it's getting hard to find that new information! Again, give your questions to a friend to answer.

Step 6

As you have been doing the puzzles, your brain has been actively searching for new information. Now write a NEW LIST that contains only the new information you have discovered when doing the puzzles. Your new list is the one to look at repeatedly for short bursts over the next few days. Try to remember more and more of it without looking at it. After a few days, you should be able to add words from your second list to your first list as you increase the information in your long-term memory.

FINALLY! Be inspired...

Make a list of different revision ideas and beside each one write **THINGS I HAVE** tried, **THINGS I WILL** try and **THINGS I MIGHT** try. Don't be scared of trying something new.

And remember – "FAIL TO PREPARE AND PREPARE TO FAIL!"

Higher Computing Science

The course

Although you may have passed National 5 Computing Science, it is important to understand that the step up to Higher is demanding and may require a different approach to ensure your success. To understand a course at Higher level often requires that you fully understand one fact before you move on to the next. If you leave a lesson confused, do something about it. Read over your notes again in the evening, ask your teacher for further explanation, attend study groups, use the world wide web for research or ask your friends for help. Whichever route you take, make sure that you get into this habit early on in the year.

The exam

The Higher Computing Science course has a question paper which contains two sections and 90 marks (60% of the total mark). Approximately 50% of the marks will be awarded for questions related to *Software Design and Development*, and 50% to *Information Systems Design and Development*.

Candidates will complete the question paper in 2 hours.

Section 1 will have 20 marks and will consist of short answer questions assessing breadth of knowledge from across both Units. Most questions will have 1–2 marks.

Section 2 will have 70 marks and will consist of approximately 6–8 extended response questions, each with approximately 8–12 marks. Questions will be of a problem-solving nature rather than direct recall and will include extended descriptions and explanations.

Approximately 50% of the marks will be awarded for questions related to *Software Design and Development*. These will include questions from the following areas:

- computational constructs and concepts
- explaining code
- writing code
- standard algorithms
- data types and structures
- software development – design, testing, documentation
- types of languages
- low level operations and computer architecture.

Questions related to programming will use the form of 'pseudocode' below:

Variable types: INTEGER, REAL, BOOLEAN, CHARACTER

Structured types: ARRAY, STRING, RECORD

Subprogram: PROCEDURE, FUNCTION

System entities: DISPLAY, KEYBOARD

Assignment: SET … TO …

Conditions: IF .. THEN .. (ELSE) … END IF

Conditional repetition: WHILE … DO … END WHILE

REPEAT … UNTIL …

Fixed repetition: REPEAT … TIMES … END REPEAT

Iteration: FOR .. FROM .. TO .. DO .. END FOR

FOR EACH … FROM … DO … END FOR EACH

Input/output: RECEIVE … FROM … ,

SEND … TO … , OPEN, CLOSE, CREATE

Operations: -, +, *, /, ^, mod, &

Comparisons: =, ≠, <, <=, >, >=

Logical operators: AND, OR, NOT

Pre-defined functions: id(parameters)

If you are required to write in code then you can use any programming language with which you are familiar or write your answer in pseudocode.

Approximately 50% of the marks will be awarded for questions related to *Information System Design and Development*. These will include questions from the following areas:

- database design, structures, links and operations
- client-side and server-side coding (including HTML, CSS and Javascript)
- website design, structures and links
- coding
- media types (including file size calculations)
- information system development – purpose, features, user interface, testing
- technical implementation – hardware, software, storage, networking/connectivity
- security, legal and environmental issues.

Question types

The Computing Science exam comprises two question types:

1. Knowledge & Understanding – questions that simply ask you to write down or explain a fact or skill you have learned.

2. Problem Solving – questions where you are required to apply your knowledge to an unfamiliar scenario.

KU questions can be easily prepared for by simply memorising lots of facts. PS questions require practice. Unseen exam questions will go some way towards preparing you for PS questions but you may find that you quickly run out of new examples. Try making up your own question scenarios and swap them with a friend. Write your own programs or create a database of your own, query it and create a variety of reports from the data. You'll find that the task of making up the questions or scenarios in a problem solving context is an exercise in itself.

General advice

Remember to read the questions carefully and answer what is being asked.

Trade Names

It is never acceptable to use a company name in an answer such as Microsoft Access, Serif Web-Plus, etc. Use the generic terms such as Databases, Web-Design packages.

Conversion

If you are asked to convert a number into an 8-bit binary number make sure that your answer has 8 bits!

Technical Terminology

It is important that the correct technical terminology is used, e.g. USB Flash Drive – not USB pen, USB stick, Pen Drive or other commonly used expressions.

Units

Remember there are 1024 bytes in a Kilobyte not 1000.

- 1024 Kilobytes in a Megabyte
- 1024 Megabytes in a Gigabyte
- 1024 Gigabytes in a Terabyte

Data Structure

The data structures you are required to know at Higher are one-dimensional arrays, records and sequential files.

Memory

Many candidates confuse the RAM memory with Backing Storage. Remember RAM memory is used to store programs and data temporarily while the program is being used. The Backing Storage is used to hold programs and data permanently until you are ready to use them. When you open an application it is taken from the Backing Storage (e.g. Hard Disc Drive) and placed into RAM memory.

Technical Implementation

Use your common sense when thinking about the reasons why you would choose a particular type of hardware. Does it have to be portable? Does it require fast processing? What is the most sensible storage device? What is the best networking solution for this particular task?

Calculating Storage Requirements

When calculating the storage requirements for photographs too many candidates forget that DPI must be squared. Remember to multiply the number of bits required to store the colour – NOT the number of colours!

For example, an image measures 3 inches by 4 inches and has a resolution of 600dpi in 8 colours

= 3 x 4 x 600 x 600 x 3 (3 bits can give 8 combinations)
= 12960000 bits = 12960000/8 =1620000 bytes
= 1620000/1024 = 1582.03 Kb = 1882.03Kb / 1024
= 1.54 Mb.

Storage Devices and Cloud Storage

Candidates often confuse the three main types of storage devices.

- Magnetic – Hard Disk Drives, Floppy Disc Drives, Magnetic Tape (DAT)
- Solid State – USB Flash Drives, Solid State Hard Drives
- Optical – CD-ROM, CD-R, CD-RW, DVD-ROM, DVD-R, DVD-RW and Blu-Ray

Computers and the Law

Candidates must give the correct, full names of the appropriate laws such as the "Regulation of Investigatory Powers Act", "Computer Misuse Act", "Communications Act" and "Copyright, Design and Patents Act".

Interfaces

Many candidates forget why an interface is required. Remember an interface changes electrical voltages, changes analogue to digital, buffers data and deals with control signals.

Pre-Defined Functions

Remember that pre-defined functions are built-in sections of code that have been written and tested and are available for programmers to use. They include common functions such as Random numbers and Rounding.

Cloud – Private, Public, Hybrid

Ensure you can accurately explain the need for three types of cloud storage by describing uses of each.

Standard Algorithms

Make sure that you have a good understanding and are able to code the five standard algorithms required at Higher.

- Input Validation
- Find Maximum
- Find Minimum
- Count Occurrences
- Linear Search

Good luck!

The most pleasing results for teachers are not necessarily the students who get the A pass. It's often the students who achieve their potential, even if that is just scraping a pass. Every year teachers see a few pupils who "could have done better". Don't let that be you!

Remember that the rewards for passing Higher Computing Science are well worth it! Your pass will help you get the future you want for yourself. In the exam, be confident in your own ability. If you're not sure how to answer a question, trust your instincts and give it a go anyway, or move on quickly. Working at a reasonable pace will allow time to return to unanswered questions later. Finally, keep calm and don't panic! GOOD LUCK!

HIGHER

2015

H

National Qualifications 2015

Mark ☐

X716/76/01

Computing Science

WEDNESDAY, 6 MAY

9:00 AM – 11:00 AM

Fill in these boxes and read what is printed below.

Full name of centre

Town

Forename(s)

Surname

Number of seat

Date of birth

Day   Month   Year   Scottish candidate number

Total marks — 90

SECTION 1 — 20 marks

Attempt ALL questions.

SECTION 2 — 70 marks

Attempt ALL questions.

Show all working.

Write your answers clearly in the spaces provided in this booklet. Additional space for answers is provided at the end of this booklet. If you use this space you must clearly identify the question number you are attempting.

Use **blue** or **black** ink.

Before leaving the examination room you must give this booklet to the Invigilator; if you do not, you may lose all the marks for this paper.

SQA

MARKS | DO NOT WRITE IN THIS MARGIN

SECTION 1 — 20 marks

Attempt ALL questions

1. Convert the decimal number −120 to binary using 8 bits.   **1**

2. Tables can be related by different types of relationships. State the type of relationship between the two tables in each case below.

   (a) People and Hobbies   **1**

   _____

   (b) Jockeys and Horses in a horse race   **1**

   _____

MARKS | DO NOT WRITE IN THIS MARGIN

3. An online company uses a computer program to display particular customer records. The algorithm of this program is shown below.

```
Line 1      SET found TO false
Line 2      RECEIVE search_name FROM (STRING) KEYBOARD
Line 3      FOR counter FROM 0 TO <End Of List> DO
Line 4          IF name[counter] = search_name THEN
Line 5              SET found TO true
Line 6              SEND name[counter] & counter TO DISPLAY
Line 7          END IF
Line 8      END FOR
Line 9      IF found = false THEN
Line 10         SEND "Name not found" TO DISPLAY
Line 11     END IF
```

The following data is stored in the name array:

Jimmy, Samina, Kate, Jimmy, Adam

State the output from the above program if Jimmy is entered at line 2 from the keyboard.

2

4. One feature of a declarative language is the use of facts. Three facts are shown in lines one to three below:

```
Line 1      human(einstein).
Line 2      human(pascal).
Line 3      human(lovelace).

Line 4      mortal(X):-human(X).
```

State the feature being used in line 4 and explain a benefit of its use.

2

[Turn over

MARKS | DO NOT WRITE IN THIS MARGIN

5. A business is setting up a new communications network.   Describe two implications of the Regulation of Investigatory Powers Act (2000) for this business.

2

_____

_____

_____

_____

6. Innes regularly uses a shopping website called Better Shop.

BETTER SHOP

Hello Innes, welcome back and what are you searching for today?

[   ]   **Search**

Items recommended to you:

Date: Wednesday 6th May 2015   Time: 21:33

Scripting is used to generate parts of the website.

(a) State **one** part of the website that is generated using client-side scripting.

1

_____

_____

(b) State **one** part of the website that is generated using server-side scripting.

1

_____

_____

MARKS | DO NOT WRITE IN THIS MARGIN

7. Craig has been asked to write an algorithm that will search for a target ID from a list of fifty receipts. Each receipt has a unique receipt ID. Part of the algorithm is shown below.

Line 1	SET found TO false
Line 2	SET counter TO −1
Line 3	RECEIVE target_id FROM (INTEGER) BARCODEREADER
Line 4	REPEAT
Line 5	SET counter TO counter + 1
Line 6	IF receipt_id [counter] = target_id THEN
Line 7	SET found TO true
Line 8	END IF
Line 9	UNTIL _____

Using pseudocode, or a language with which you are familiar, complete line 9 of the algorithm shown above.

2

8. Describe **two** benefits of prototyping when following a rapid application development methodology.

2

9. Explain how cache memory can improve system performance.

2

[Turn over

MARKS | DO NOT WRITE IN THIS MARGIN

10. Describe how usability testing could be carried out on a website.

2

_____

_____

_____

_____

11. A database table may have a compound key. State what is meant by the term compound key.

1

_____

_____

[Turn over for SECTION 2 on *Page eight*]

DO NOT WRITE ON THIS PAGE

SECTION 2 — 70 marks

Attempt ALL questions

12. A hardware company uses a relational database with the four tables shown below.

Customer	Item	Order	Sale
Customer ID	*Item ID*	*Order no*	Order no *
Customer name	Description	Customer ID *	Item ID *
Customer address	Cost	Date	Quantity
Customer email	Image		

(a) Identify a suitable primary key for the **Sale** table.

1

_____

(b) Draw an *entity-relationship diagram* to illustrate the relationships between the four tables.

3

MARKS | DO NOT WRITE IN THIS MARGIN

12.   (continued)

(c) A report is produced each time a customer makes an order. An example is shown below.

Customer	Mr D Gryffe	Order no	10728
	12 Gourock Crescent	Date	23/4/15

Item	Number ordered	Cost
Grease spray	1	£6·99
Bell wire (100 m)	1	£8·50
Towel radiator	1	£121·50
Disposable mouse trap	2	£9·98
	Total	£146·97

This report is based on a query. State a list of the tables and fields that would be used in this query and any criteria that would be used to select the above data.   3

(d) The report includes a single total of £146·97 after the four subtotals. Describe how this can be done in the report.   3

[Turn over

MARKS | DO NOT WRITE IN THIS MARGIN

13. EcoCaledonia are an energy company based in Scotland. Sales representatives visit people's houses in an attempt to gain business from new customers.

The sales representatives take a tablet device and often show video clips using apps and mobile websites.

(a) Describe how quad-core processors can be used to improve load times for web apps containing client-side scripts or multimedia.　　2

_____

_____

_____

_____

(b) Describe how compression reduces the file size of videos.　　3

_____

_____

_____

_____

_____

_____

MARKS | DO NOT WRITE IN THIS MARGIN

13.   (continued)

(c)   EcoCaledonia plan to launch an app that will allow customers with Internet access to turn their heating system on using a mobile device.

Describe how EcoCaledonia could ensure that all customers could use the software regardless of the operating system on their device.   **2**

_____

_____

_____

_____

(d)   Customers of EcoCaledonia can sign in to their account to supply meter readings, pay bills and update contact details.

Explain how their details are secure when transmitted.   **3**

_____

_____

_____

_____

_____

_____

[Turn over

MARKS | DO NOT WRITE IN THIS MARGIN

13. (continued)

(e) When signing in to their account customers have to enter details from their username and password as shown below.

> **Your username**
> Enter the following characters from your username
>
> Enter the 3rd character   [•]
>
> Enter the 4th character   [•]
>
> Enter the 1st character   [•]
>
> **Your password**
> Enter the following characters from your password
>
> Enter the 3rd character   [•]
>
> Enter the 4th character   [•]
>
> Enter the 1st character   [•]
>
> ⬅ ➡

Explain why customers are asked to enter their details in a random order each time.   1

_____

_____

[Turn over for Question 14 on *Page fourteen*]

DO NOT WRITE ON THIS PAGE

MARKS | DO NOT WRITE IN THIS MARGIN

14. EcoCaledonia recruits employees using an online application form. Rowena completes her form and receives the feedback below:

Please correct the following information

* Indicates required fields

Title: *　　　　　　　　　Miss ▼

First name: *　　　　　　　Rowena

Surname: *　　　　　　　　Drayton

Gender: *　　　　　　　　○ Male　◉ Female

Email address: *　　　　　　rowenadrayton@schoolmail.co.uk

Mobile phone number:　　　077g6367324

　　　　　　　　　　　　　Please enter a valid mobile phone number

Are you happy to receive information from our partner companies　☑

(a) State the most appropriate data type used to store the value of the "receive information" check box.　　　1

_____

(b) Rowena accidentally entered an invalid mobile phone number and an error message is displayed. A valid mobile phone number will consist of a string of 11 digits.

Using pseudocode or a programming language of your choice, write the algorithm which would check that the mobile phone number is valid.　　　5

MARKS | DO NOT WRITE IN THIS MARGIN

14.   (continued)

(c)   An algorithm is implemented to validate the applicant's data from the application form opposite. There are two subprograms at lines two and three. The parameters for these subprograms are not shown.

Line 1   REPEAT Line 2   Enter_applicant_data (…) Line 3   Validate_form_data (…) Line 4   UNTIL <form data is valid>

Name a parameter that should be passed at line 2, state the type of parameter passing used and justify your answer.

2

_____

_____

_____

_____

(d)   EcoCaledonia has its own servers which need to be upgraded and is considering migrating to a hybrid cloud.

(i)   Describe what is meant by a hybrid cloud.

1

_____

_____

(ii)   State **two** advantages for EcoCaledonia of switching to a hybrid cloud.

2

_____

_____

_____

_____

[Turn over

MARKS | DO NOT WRITE IN THIS MARGIN

15. A local hair salon has a desktop computer, a tablet computer and a printer. These devices are networked using a wireless connection.

(a) The hair salon needs to use software that is only available for an older operating system. State how the hair salon could run this software on their system.

1

_____

_____

(b) Staff can access all files on the network. Customers can only access a catalogue file of various hair styles. Describe how the operating system allows these restrictions to be set up.

2

_____

_____

_____

_____

(c) A digital camera is used to take the customer's photograph and then the camera is connected to the desktop computer using an interface.

(i) State **two** tasks undertaken by an interface when transferring these photographs to the desktop computer.

2

_____

_____

_____

_____

(ii) The photograph can then be edited so that the customer can view it with a range of hair styles and colours. This photograph could be a bitmap or vector graphic. Select one type of graphic and explain why it is suitable for this purpose.

2

_____

_____

_____

_____

MARKS | DO NOT WRITE IN THIS MARGIN

15.   (continued)

(d) The hair salon also has some video clips stored on their computer that they use to train staff.

Calculate the uncompressed file size of one of these video clips which is 90 seconds long and was captured at 25 frames per second with a resolution of 260 by 200 pixels and 16 777 216 colours.

State your answer in appropriate units and show all working.   **2**

(e) The manager of the hair salon is considering whether to buy new computers or to upgrade the existing ones.

(i) Describe **one** environmental advantage of upgrading.   **1**

_____

_____

(ii) Describe **one** environmental advantage of buying new computers.   **1**

_____

_____

[Turn over

MARKS

16. Joseph has been asked to develop a website for the Glasburgh Safari Park where visitors can go to see animals including pandas. Joseph often makes use of cascading style sheets which can be internal or external.

(a) Describe the difference between an internal style sheet and an external style sheet.

2

_____

_____

_____

_____

(b) Explain why the use of external style sheets may result in optimal load times when compared to the use of internal style sheets.

2

_____

_____

_____

_____

(c) Joseph is using an external style sheet named "masterstyle". Complete the HTML code that will successfully link to this stylesheet.

2

```
<link rel = _____ type= "text/css" href= _____>
```

(d) Joseph includes a rule in the external style sheet to make all the large headings appear in Tahoma font, blue and centred wherever they appear on each page.

Write a CSS rule to manage these large headings.

3

MARKS | DO NOT WRITE IN THIS MARGIN

16. (continued)

(e) Searching for the 'Glasburgh Safari' or 'pandas' on the World Wide Web with a search engine does not give a prominent result for this site. Describe **two** ways that Joseph can improve this without incurring any further costs.

2

_____

_____

_____

_____

(f) Customers can purchase tickets via the website.

Explain how the use of a database driven website would allow the safari park to display a message if there were only a small number of tickets left on a certain day.

2

_____

_____

_____

_____

[Turn over

MARKS | DO NOT WRITE IN THIS MARGIN

17. Chris wants a program to process information about each of the pupils in his class.

Line 1	RECORD Test_marks IS {STRING surname, INTEGER mark_1, INTEGER mark_2, INTEGER mark_3, STRING email}
Line 2	SET pupil[1] TO ("Smith", 67, 89, 91, "john@doodle.co.uk")
Line 3	SET pupil[2] TO ("Latif", 42, 91, 84, "fatima@doodle.co.uk")
Line 4	SEND pupil[1].mark_2 TO DISPLAY

(a) (i) Explain the purpose of line 2.   2

_____

_____

_____

_____

(ii) State the output from line 4.   1

_____

_____

(iii) Chris wants to calculate the average for the first pupil. Using pseudocode, or a language with which you are familiar, write the line to calculate this average.   2

MARKS | DO NOT WRITE IN THIS MARGIN

17. **(continued)**

(b) Chris calculates the average mark for each pupil and stores the average marks in an array. He writes the following pseudocode to count the number of grade A passes of 70 or more:

```
Line 1      SET list TO [74.33, 57.67, 73.33, 82.33]
Line 2      SET amount TO 0
Line 3      FOR counter FROM 0 TO 2 DO
Line 4            IF list[counter] >= 70 THEN
Line 5                  SET amount TO amount + 1
Line 6            END IF
Line 7      END FOR
Line 8      SEND amount TO DISPLAY
```

When Chris tests the program, it outputs the wrong number of A passes.

(i) State the output from the code above.　　　　　　　　　　　1

_____

(ii) State the name of this type of error.　　　　　　　　　　　1

_____

(iii) Identify and correct the line of the algorithm which contains the error.　　　　　　　　　　　2

[Turn over for Question 17(c) on *Page twenty-two*

MARKS | DO NOT WRITE IN THIS MARGIN

17. (continued)

(c) Chris creates an algorithm that will search the array of average marks and return the smallest value present.

```
Line 1 SET list to [74.33, 57.67, 73.33, 87.33]
Line 2 SET minimum TO list [0]
Line 3 FOR counter FROM 1 TO 3 DO
Line 4    IF minimum > list[counter] THEN
Line 5        SET minimum TO list[counter]
Line 6    END IF
Line 7 END FOR
```

A trace table is used to record the change to a variable at the corresponding line number. Part of the trace table is shown below. State the values missing from the trace table below at A, B and C.

Line	list	minimum	counter
1	74.33, 57.67, 73.33, 87.33		
2		A	
3			B
5		C	
3	....	....	....

3

A _____

B _____

C _____

(d) Explain how breakpoints could be used in conjunction with a trace table to locate errors in code.

2

_____

_____

_____

_____

[END OF QUESTION PAPER]

ADDITIONAL SPACE FOR ANSWERS

ADDITIONAL SPACE FOR ANSWERS

MARKS DO NOT WRITE IN THIS MARGIN

ADDITIONAL SPACE FOR ANSWERS

HIGHER

2016

H

National
Qualifications
2016

Mark

X716/76/01

Computing Science

FRIDAY, 27 MAY

1:00 PM — 3:00 PM

Fill in these boxes and read what is printed below.

Full name of centre

Town

Forename(s)

Surname

Number of seat

Date of birth
Day   Month   Year   Scottish candidate number

Total marks — 90

SECTION 1 — 20 marks

Attempt ALL questions.

SECTION 2 — 70 marks

Attempt ALL questions.

Show all working.

Write your answers clearly in the spaces provided in this booklet. Additional space for answers is provided at the end of this booklet. If you use this space you must clearly identify the question number you are attempting.

Use **blue** or **black** ink.

Before leaving the examination room you must give this booklet to the Invigilator; if you do not, you may lose all the marks for this paper.

MARKS | DO NOT WRITE IN THIS MARGIN

SECTION 1 — 20 marks

Attempt ALL questions

1. A real number is stored using 32-bit floating point representation. The mantissa is allocated 24 bits and 8 bits are allocated to the exponent.

   Describe the effect if the allocation is changed to a 16-bit mantissa and a 16-bit exponent.

   2

   _____

   _____

   _____

   _____

2. Nadia wishes to store a video clip that is 24 frames per second, duration is 95 seconds and has a resolution of 1280 × 720 with a colour depth of 16 bits.

   Calculate the storage requirement for the uncompressed video clip. Show all working and express your answer in appropriate units.

   2

MARKS | DO NOT WRITE IN THIS MARGIN

3. Classes and subclasses are key characteristics of object-oriented programming.

Explain why the use of classes and subclasses reduces implementation time for programmers.

2

_____

_____

_____

_____

_____

_____

_____

4. Rapid Application Development (RAD) is often used when a program is required quickly.

Describe **two** ways that the use of Rapid Application Development (RAD) reduces the time taken to create a working program.

2

_____

_____

_____

_____

_____

_____

[Turn over

MARKS | DO NOT WRITE IN THIS MARGIN

5. An administrator at a gym uses a database to add new member details. Members can have student, adult or senior membership. The administrator types new member details into a form as shown below.

MEMBER DETAILS

First Name:	Oliver
Last Name:	Wilson
D.O.B.:	21/01/1994
Member ID:	3133
Membership:	Student

Describe **two** ways to improve the usability of this form.   2

_____

_____

_____

_____

_____

_____

6. Pupils access files from a shared folder on their school network server. These files are available for the pupils to open, but only a teacher can edit and save the files to this folder.

Describe how this is implemented.　2

7. BorrowABike is a company that hires bikes to customers for one day. They have a relational database with three tables as shown below.

Members	Bikes	Hire
MemberID	BikeID	MemberID*
Name	Colour	BikeID*
Address	Wheelsize	HireDate
Phone		Cost

(a) Explain why a compound key is required for the Hire table.　1

(b) The data dictionary for a table includes the field name. State **two** other items that would be specified in a data dictionary.　2

MARKS | DO NOT WRITE IN THIS MARGIN

8. A website containing information about different countries is being created. Part of the HTML code is shown below.

```
<html>
<head>
        <title><h1>Countries</h1></title>
<head>
<body>
        <h1> Welcome to countries of the world!</h1>
        <p1>Countries in Europe</p1>
        <p align = centre> France</p>
</body>
</html>
```

(a) Identify **two** errors in the HTML code above.   2

_____

_____

(b) The developer of the website decides to include metatags.

(i) State the purpose of metatags.   1

_____

_____

_____

(ii) State where in the code the metatags should be inserted.   1

_____

_____

_____

9. State **one** reason why the increased use of technology has had a negative effect on the environment.   1

_____

_____

_____

MARKS | DO NOT WRITE IN THIS MARGIN

SECTION 2 — 70 marks

Attempt ALL questions

10. Mrs McColl is a computing teacher who creates a program to grade her pupils' work. Mrs McColl's students have had two tests, one in Software Design and Development (SDD) and one in Information Systems Design and Development (ISDD).

Name	SDD	ISDD
Liam	C	B
Sohale	D	C
Craig	A	A
Katya	B	B
Rebecca	B	C
Wei-Lin	B	B

(a) Using pseudocode, or a programming language of your choice, write an algorithm for a subroutine that will count the number of pupils who achieved a grade B in both tests.   5

[Turn over

MARKS | DO NOT WRITE IN THIS MARGIN

10. (continued)

(b) Mrs McColl implements the program using global variables. Another teacher suggests that she makes use of parameter passing instead.

State **two** benefits of using parameter passing rather than global variables.

2

_____

_____

_____

_____

_____

_____

Parameters are used to pass data between subprograms. Parameters can be passed by reference or passed by value.

(c) Explain why passing by value is more demanding on system resources when the data being passed is held in an array.

2

_____

_____

_____

_____

_____

_____

MARKS | DO NOT WRITE IN THIS MARGIN

10.   **(continued)**

(d)   Mrs McColl's program is modular and makes use of functions. Explain what is meant by a function.   **1**

_____

_____

_____

_____

(e)   Mrs McColl's employer must conform with the requirements of the Regulation of Investigatory Powers Act (RIPA).

    (i)   State **two** responsibilities, detailed in this act, for the employer.   **2**

_____

_____

_____

_____

_____

_____

    (ii)   Describe **two** concerns Mrs McColl may have as a result of this act.   **2**

_____

_____

_____

_____

_____

_____

[Turn over

MARKS | DO NOT WRITE IN THIS MARGIN

11. Tomek has created a website for the fans of the China Cats electropop group. The site has a home page at www.tomek91.com with links to three pages: a Tour Dates page, a Band Members page and a Fans page.

(a) Describe an addition that would make this a multi-level site.   1

_____

_____

_____

(b) On the Band Members page, when the pointer is moved over the name of each member a photograph and a mini-biography are shown.

This interactive feature was created using a scripting language. Describe how this is executed.   1

_____

_____

_____

(c) Tomek was asked to make all the large headings appear in Tahoma font, blue and centred wherever they appear on each page. He chooses to do this with an external style sheet.

(i) Write a Cascading Style Sheet (CSS) rule to manage the large headings.   3

MARKS | DO NOT WRITE IN THIS MARGIN

11. (c) (continued)

    (ii) State **two** benefits of using an external style sheet.   2

  (d) Searching for the "China Cats" or "electropop" on the World Wide Web with a search engine does not give a prominent result for this site.

    Describe **two** ways that Tomek can improve this without incurring any further costs.   2

  (e) Tomek is planning to sell band merchandise through his website.

    Explain why the presence of a digital certificate will improve customer confidence when buying from the website.   2

[Turn over

MARKS | DO NOT WRITE IN THIS MARGIN

12. Emma works in a recording studio. She needs a music mixing program that supports all the latest audio file formats.

(a) Emma can choose between open source or proprietary software.

Describe a benefit, to Emma, of each type of software.

2

_____

_____

_____

_____

_____

(b) Emma would also like to use the music software on her home computer. Her home computer has an operating system which is not compatible with her choice of software.

Describe a software solution that would allow Emma to run the program on her current operating system.

2

_____

_____

_____

_____

_____

(c) Emma records a vocalist singing the voice track for a new recording.

(i) Describe how increasing the sample rate and depth at the time of recording would improve the quality of this sound file.

2

_____

_____

_____

_____

_____

MARKS | DO NOT WRITE IN THIS MARGIN

12. (c) (continued)

(ii) Describe a compression technique that reduces the file size for sound.

1

_____

_____

_____

_____

(d) Emma's home computer has a data bus and an address bus.

Describe how each bus is used when reading data from memory.

2

_____

_____

_____

_____

_____

_____

[Turn over

13. Eloïse wants to search for an item of data held in an array. She writes the following algorithm.

```
Line 1      SET list to [71,76,66,67,89,72]
Line 2      SET target to 71
Line 3      SET found to false
Line 4      FOR counter FROM 0 to 5 DO
Line 5          IF list[counter]=target THEN
Line 6              SET found to true
Line 7          ELSE
Line 8              SET found to false
LINE 9          END IF
LINE 10     END FOR
LINE 11     IF found =true THEN
LINE 12         SEND "Item found" TO DISPLAY
LINE 13     ELSE
LINE 14         SEND "Not found" TO DISPLAY
LINE 15     END IF
```

(a) A trace table is shown below which shows the line numbers where a variable has changed. State the missing values at A, B, C and D

Line	list	target	counter	found
1	[71,76,66,67,89,72]			
2		A		
3				B
4			0	
6				C
4			1	
8				D

A = _____ B = _____ C = _____ D = _____   4

(b) The algorithm is incorrect and so outputs the wrong message.

   (i) Explain why the algorithm is incorrect.   1

   _____

   _____

   _____

MARKS | DO NOT WRITE IN THIS MARGIN

13. **(b) (continued)**

    (ii) Describe how to correct the algorithm.   **1**

_____

_____

_____

_____

  (c) Explain why the use of cache memory improves system performance when running lines 4 to 10.   **2**

_____

_____

_____

_____

_____

_____

[Turn over

MARKS | DO NOT WRITE IN THIS MARGIN

14. Isnaeworld is a theme park in Harris. It uses a database driven website. On any given day, there are 5000 entry tickets available.

(a) State **two** reasons why Isnaeworld makes use of a database driven website.

2

_____

_____

_____

_____

14. **(continued)**

(b) Customers can purchase tickets to gain entry to the theme park by completing an online form.

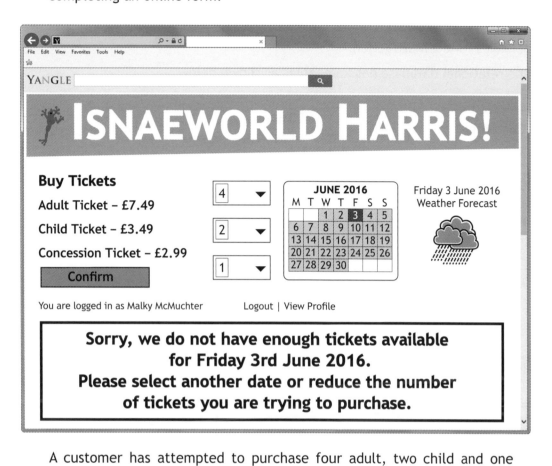

A customer has attempted to purchase four adult, two child and one concession tickets.

Explain how the web server dynamically generates the web page shown above.

4

14.   (continued)

(c)   Isnaeworld also allows customers to book tickets for specific attractions within the theme park. Isnaeworld uses a relational database to store bookings for each attraction.

The relational database has four tables as shown below.

Customer	Attraction Booking	Theme Park	Attraction
Customer ID	Customer ID*	Park ID	Attraction ID
First Name	Attraction ID*	Name	Park ID*
Surname	Card Number	Town	Manufacturer
Member Status	Ref Number	Postcode	Category
	Date		

Draw an entity relationship diagram to show the relationships between the four tables.   3

MARKS | DO NOT WRITE IN THIS MARGIN

14. **(continued)**

(d) Isnaeworld make a full backup of all of their data every Sunday.

    (i) Explain why this backup strategy is insufficient.   **1**

_____

_____

_____

    (ii) Describe how this backup strategy could be improved.   **2**

_____

_____

_____

_____

_____

_____

(e) When a customer attempts to buy tickets on the Isnaeworld website, they see the following message and check box.

> By ticking this box you give us permission to share your details with third party organisations
>
> ✓   Accept

Explain why Isnaeworld must include this message if they intend to share customer details with third party organisations.   **2**

_____

_____

_____

_____

_____

MARKS | DO NOT WRITE IN THIS MARGIN

15. Tony coaches a team of eight elite athletes for a 400 metre race. Tony uses a program to help analyse each athlete's performance.

A sample of the data held on each athlete is shown below.

Athlete Data	
Forename	Salma
Surname	Hussain
Runner number	324
Professional	True
Season best	45·12
Weight (kg)	67·5

Tony has added a record structure to his program.

RECORD athleteData IS {STRING forename, STRING surname, INTEGER runnerNumber, BOOLEAN professional, REAL seasonBest, REAL weight}

(a) Tony wants to store his eight athletes' data using the record structure shown above. The variable name is athletes.

Using pseudocode, or a programming language of your choice, declare the variable which can store the data for the eight athletes.

2

(b) Using pseudocode, or a programming language of your choice, write the code necessary to add the data for the athlete Salma shown in the table above. Your answer should use the variable declared in part (a).

3

MARKS | DO NOT WRITE IN THIS MARGIN

15.   (continued)

(c) Tony wants to find the fastest 400 m time of the season.

Using pseudocode, or a programming language of your choice, design an algorithm to find the fastest season time. Your answer should use the variable declared in part (a).   5

MARKS | DO NOT WRITE IN THIS MARGIN

15. **(continued)**

(d) Tony has added the following to his program.

Line 1   CREATE "C:\MyAthletes\winner.txt"
Line 2   SEND fastest TO "C:\MyAthletes\winner.txt"
Line 3   CLOSE "C:\MyAthletes\winner.txt"

(i) Describe the purpose of line 1.   1

_____

_____

_____

(ii) Describe the purpose of line 2.   1

_____

_____

_____

(e) Tony runs his program but the program produces the wrong output when compared with his test data.

Other than a trace table, name and describe a technique that Tony could use to locate and identify the error.   2

_____

_____

_____

_____

_____

_____

_____

[END OF QUESTION PAPER]

MARKS | DO NOT WRITE IN THIS MARGIN

ADDITIONAL SPACE FOR ANSWERS

ADDITIONAL SPACE FOR ANSWERS

HIGHER

2017

National
Qualifications
2017

Mark

X716/76/01

Computing Science

TUESDAY, 16 MAY

1:00 PM – 3:00 PM

Fill in these boxes and read what is printed below.

Full name of centre

Town

Forename(s)

Surname

Number of seat

Date of birth

Day	Month	Year

Scottish candidate number

Total marks — 90

SECTION 1 — 20 marks

Attempt ALL questions.

SECTION 2 — 70 marks

Attempt ALL questions.

Show all workings.

Write your answers clearly in the spaces provided in this booklet. Additional space for answers is provided at the end of this booklet. If you use this space you must clearly identify the question number you are attempting.

Use **blue** or **black** ink.

Before leaving the examination room you must give this booklet to the Invigilator; if you do not, you may lose all the marks for this paper.

MARKS | DO NOT WRITE IN THIS MARGIN

SECTION 1 — 20 marks

Attempt ALL questions

1. State the range of positive and negative numbers that can be represented using 16 bit two's complement representation.

2

2. Describe the analysis stage of the software development process.

2

3. A stereo sound file lasting 2 minutes with a sample rate of 96 kHz and sample depth of 16 bits is stored on a computer.

    Calculate the storage size of the uncompressed sound file.

    Show all working and express your answer in appropriate units.

3

MARKS | DO NOT WRITE IN THIS MARGIN

4. Tables within a database can make use of compound keys and surrogate keys.

Explain the difference between a compound key and a surrogate key.

2

_____

_____

_____

_____

_____

5. Tracking cookies can be created and used when browsing a website.

Describe a security risk associated with tracking cookies.

1

_____

_____

_____

_____

6. Customers log into their bank account using a username, PIN and password.

Explain how public and private keys help to keep these details secure when transmitted between the customer and the bank's server.

2

_____

_____

_____

_____

_____

MARKS | DO NOT WRITE IN THIS MARGIN

7. There are many disabilities or impairments that can be a barrier to effective computer use.

   (a) Visual impairments could be overcome by using large fonts.

   State one other feature that could help a person with a visual impairment.

   1

   _____

   _____

   _____

   _____

   (b) Hearing impairments could be overcome by adjusting the speaker volume.

   State one other feature that could help a person with a hearing impairment.

   1

   _____

   _____

   _____

   _____

8. Describe how object-oriented languages are used to create software.

   2

   _____

   _____

   _____

   _____

   _____

   _____

   _____

MARKS | DO NOT WRITE IN THIS MARGIN

9. A programmer is creating a program to store details about books. The details stored are: title, author, number of pages and price.

(a) Create, using pseudocode or a language with which you are familiar, a record structure to store the book details.

2

(b) Declare, using pseudocode or a language with which you are familiar, a variable that can store the data for 1000 books.

2

[END OF SECTION 1]

[Turn over

MARKS | DO NOT WRITE IN THIS MARGIN

SECTION 2 — 70 MARKS

Attempt ALL Questions

10. HiDoe manufactures intelligent heating control systems that allow users to monitor the temperature in different rooms in their house. An app can be downloaded to access information about energy use.

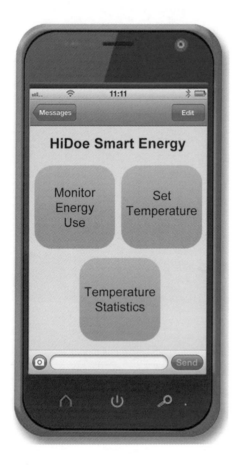

Selecting **Temperature Statistics** on the app allows users to see the highest and lowest temperature of a room over the course of a 24 hour period.

A sensor measures the temperature in a room at the start of each hour in a day. These temperatures are stored in an array called `temps`.

index	0	1	2	3	....	22	23
temps	10	8	12	11	....	14	13

MARKS | DO NOT WRITE IN THIS MARGIN

10. **(continued)**

(a) The temperature statistics feature displays the message:

The lowest temperature was 8 Celsius at hour 1.

Write, using pseudocode or a language with which you are familiar, an algorithm that can:

- find the lowest temperature

- display the message shown above

- write the lowest temperature to an external file called "low.txt".

7

(b) Name a function of the operating system and describe one task it will perform when creating the external file.

2

_____

_____

_____

_____

_____

10. **(continued)**

The app makes use of a function to calculate the average.

Line 1   FUNCTION calcAverage (ARRAY OF INTEGER list) RETURNS INTEGER
Line 2   DECLARE total AS INTEGER INITIALLY 0
Line 3   DECLARE average AS INTEGER INITIALLY 0
Line 4   FOR index FROM 0 TO 23 DO
Line 5   SET total TO total + list[index]
Line 6   SET average TO total / (index +1)
Line 7   END FOR
Line 8   RETURN average
Line 9   END FUNCTION

MARKS | DO NOT WRITE IN THIS MARGIN

(c) At the end of the first iteration, the values for total and average are both 10.

   (i) Complete the following trace table to show the values of the total and average variables at the end of the *second and third iteration* of the loop.

2

End of Iteration	Total	Average
1	10	10
2		
3		

   (ii) On the fourth iteration, a runtime error occurs. Error reporting states that line 6 is the cause.

   Explain why this line causes the problem and how to correct it.

2

_____

_____

_____

_____

_____

MARKS | DO NOT WRITE IN THIS MARGIN

10. (continued)

(d) The calcAverage function only works for 24 integers.

Describe how the function could be altered to calculate the average for any size of list.

1

_____

_____

_____

_____

_____

(e) Describe two ways that intelligent heating systems such as HiDoe can be used to reduce the carbon footprint of homes.

2

_____

_____

_____

_____

_____

_____

_____

_____

[Turn over

11. Super Taxi allows users to book taxis from their smartphones. Super Taxi uses a relational database to keep a record of their cars, drivers, bookings and customers.

Each driver can only drive one car but the same car can be used by more than one driver. The cost is set at the time of booking.

Car	Driver	Booking	Customer
<u>Registration</u>	<u>Driver ID</u>	<u>Booking ID</u>	<u>Customer ID</u>
Make	First Name	From	Known As
Model	Surname	To	Card Number
Licence Expires	Mobile	Cost	Expiry Date
	Registration*	Driver ID*	Authorisation Code
		Customer ID*	

(a) Draw an entity relationship diagram to show the relationships between the four tables.

3

11. (continued)

MARKS | DO NOT WRITE IN THIS MARGIN

(b) A query is used to generate the report shown below. This report is displayed on a customer's smartphone once a booking is confirmed.

(i) State the tables and fields needed to generate the above report.   3

_____

_____

_____

_____

_____

_____

_____

_____

(ii) State the search criteria that would identify this booking.   1

_____

MARKS | DO NOT WRITE IN THIS MARGIN

11. (continued)

The following is an extract from the source code used to generate Super Taxi's homepage.

```
<!DOCTYPE html>
<html>
    <head>
        <title>Super Taxi</title>
    </head>

    <body>

        <h1  id="welcome" onmouseover="mouseOver()"
            onmouseout="mouseOut()">Welcome to Super Taxi</h1>

        <script>
            function mouseOver() {
                document.getElementById("welcome").style.color = "yellow";
            }
            function mouseOut() {
                document.getElementById("welcome").style.color = "black";
            }
        </script>

    </body>
</html>
```

(c) Explain, making reference to the code shown above, what happens when a user places the mouse pointer over the heading "Welcome to Super Taxi".   2

_____

_____

_____

_____

(d) Meta tags can be used in this webpage.

Insert the missing components of the following meta tag:

<meta _____="keywords" _____="super, taxi">   2

11.   (continued)

(e)   Search engine providers realised that web developers were placing large numbers of keywords in meta tags to improve a website's ranking in search results. This means that meta tags are often ignored by search engines.

Describe two techniques that search engines use to ensure more relevant results are returned.

2

(f)   The following line of code is added to the homepage:

`<link rel="stylesheet" type= "text/css" href= "superstyle.css">`

State the section of the code in which this line should be placed.

1

(g)   Describe the effect on efficiency of web page load times when comparing external and internal CSS.

2

12. A program is used to calculate parking charges for a public car park.

The arrival and departure times are converted to and stored as real numbers, for example: 06:30 hours will be converted to and stored as 6.5.

Welcome to Shore Car Park

CHARGES	all charges include VAT
UP TO 1 HOUR	£2·75
UP TO 2 HOURS	£4·25
OVER 2 HOURS	£6·25

The function below is used to calculate the cost of parking for each car.

```
Line 1      FUNCTION calcCost(REAL departure, REAL arrival) RETURNS REAL
Line 1          DECLARE hours_parked INITIALLY 0
Line 3          DECLARE parking_charge INITIALLY 0
Line 4          SET hours_parked TO departure – arrival
Line 5          IF hours_parked <= 1 THEN
Line 6              SET parking_charge TO 2.75
Line 7          ELSE
Line 8              IF hours_parked <=2 THEN
Line 9                  SET parking_charge TO 4.25
Line 10             ELSE
Line 11                 SET parking_charge TO 6.25
Line 12             END IF
Line 13         END IF
Line 14         RETURN parking_charge
Line 15     END FUNCTION
```

This function is called using the line below:

SET cost TO calcCost (arrived, left)

MARKS | DO NOT WRITE IN THIS MARGIN

(a) Identify a formal parameter used in the code above and explain what is meant by a formal parameter.

2

MARKS | DO NOT WRITE IN THIS MARGIN

12. **(continued)**

(b) A car arrived at the car park at 10:00 and left at 13:00.

When the function is called, arrived has the value 10.0 and left has the value 13.0. The function returns an incorrect cost of 2.75.

Explain why this function did not return the expected value.   **2**

_____

_____

_____

_____

_____

_____

_____

(c) Watchpoints are often used during testing.

Describe how watchpoints are used to help programmers locate errors.   **2**

_____

_____

_____

_____

(d) The function makes use of a local variable.

Describe two benefits of using local variables.   **2**

_____

_____

_____

_____

_____

_____

MARKS | DO NOT WRITE IN THIS MARGIN

13. PCBits is an online shopping site which sells computer hardware and software.

The diagram below shows a proposed version of their new website.

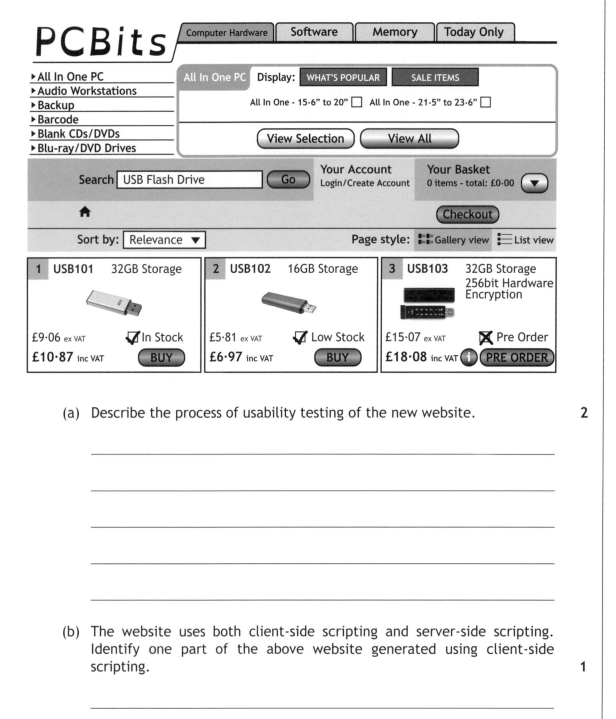

(a) Describe the process of usability testing of the new website.　　2

_____

_____

_____

_____

_____

(b) The website uses both client-side scripting and server-side scripting. Identify one part of the above website generated using client-side scripting.　　1

_____

_____

MARKS | DO NOT WRITE IN THIS MARGIN

13. **(continued)**

(c) Explain how the use of a database driven website would allow the PCBits website to display a message stating whether items are In Stock, Low Stock or available for Pre-Order.

3

| £9·06 ex VAT   ✓ In Stock | £5·81 ex VAT   ✓ Low Stock | £15·07 ex VAT   ✗ Pre Order |
| £10·87 inc VAT ⓘ BUY | £6·97 inc VAT ⓘ BUY | £18·08 inc VAT ⓘ PRE ORDER |

_____

_____

_____

_____

_____

(d) PCBits is concerned about a loss of data such as customer details and orders.

(i) Describe a suitable backup schedule for PCBits. Your answer should include a description of the type of backup.

2

_____

_____

_____

_____

_____

_____

(ii) Describe one other strategy that could be used to protect against a loss of data.

1

_____

_____

_____

_____

[Turn over

MARKS | DO NOT WRITE IN THIS MARGIN

13. **(continued)**

(e) The code for one of the webpages is shown below:

```
<!DOCTYPE html>
<html>
      <head>
            <style>
                  p{color:red; text-align: center}
            </style>
      </head>

      <body>
            <p> Welcome To </p>
            <p style="color:blue; font-size:200%;"> PCBits</p>
            <p> Glasgow </p>
      </body>
</html>
```

Describe the output from this code. You may use a labelled diagram to support your answer.

2

MARKS | DO NOT WRITE IN THIS MARGIN

14. Catherine runs CraftyBella, an online business promoting arts and crafts.

(a) Catherine is concerned that the business data stored on the public cloud is not secure.

Explain why this is **not** the case.

2

_____

_____

_____

_____

(b) Catherine has designed a black and white logo. There is both a bitmapped and vector graphic of the logo shown below.

(i) Catherine wants to move the ears of the cat closer together. State whether this task is easier to do with the bitmapped or the vector graphic. Explain your answer.

2

_____

_____

_____

_____

_____

_____

_____

_____

MARKS | DO NOT WRITE IN THIS MARGIN

14. (b) (continued)

(ii) Describe the effect on the file size of adding the star to both the vector **and** bitmapped graphic.

2

_____

_____

_____

_____

MARKS | DO NOT WRITE IN THIS MARGIN

15. A manufacturer of mobile phones is considering the SnapLizard processor. A description of the SnapLizard is given below.

> The SnapLizard processor has a clock speed of 2·4 GHz. It is quad core, resulting in extremely efficient multi-tasking when compared to dual core processors. The data bus and the address bus are both 32 bits. The SnapLizard includes a separate instruction and data cache.

(a) The processor runs the machine code version of an application by fetching and executing instructions from memory. Describe the steps of the fetch-execute cycle.

3

(b) The SnapLizard includes cache for instructions and data.

   (i) Explain how cache improves performance.

2

[Turn over

MARKS | DO NOT WRITE IN THIS MARGIN

15. (b) (continued)

(ii) The SnapLizard has many registers including X and Y registers. Here are three low level language instructions that are fetched and executed in sequence:

1	LOAD X, 2000	Loads the contents of memory location with address 2000 into the X register.
2	LOAD Y, 2000	Loads the contents of memory location with address 2000 into the Y register.
3	ADD X, Y	Add the contents of the Y register to the X register.

Explain the impact of cache on the execution of instructions 2 and 3.   **2**

(c) The mobile phone should be capable of capturing high quality video.

One characteristic that would be considered would be bit depth. Describe the difference between a bit depth of 16 bits and that of 24 bits for the quality of video.   **2**

MARKS | DO NOT WRITE IN THIS MARGIN

15. **(continued)**

(d) (i) Describe how video is compressed using interframe and intraframe compression.   2

_____

_____

_____

_____

_____

(ii) The effectiveness of video compression can depend on the content that is being captured. For example, videoing someone sitting singing a song on stage will compress differently when compared to videoing a high energy dance performance with a group of dancers.

Explain the effectiveness of interframe compression for these different performances.   2

_____

_____

_____

_____

_____

_____

_____

_____

_____

[END OF QUESTION PAPER]

ADDITIONAL SPACE FOR ANSWERS

MARKS | DO NOT WRITE IN THIS MARGIN

ADDITIONAL SPACE FOR ANSWERS

[BLANK PAGE]

DO NOT WRITE ON THIS PAGE

SQA HIGHER
COMPUTING SCIENCE 2017

HIGHER COMPUTING SCIENCE 2015

Section 1

Question			Expected Answer(s)	Max mark
1.			1000 1000 – using 8 bit 2's complement method **OR** 1111 1000 – using sign bit method	1
2.	(a)		Many to many	1
	(b)		One to one	1
3.			Jimmy 0 Jimmy 3 1 mark for Jimmy output twice Or 1 mark for Jimmy 0 Or 1 mark for Jimmy 3 2 marks for full correct answer	2
4.			Feature • Rule • Uses capital letter to identify variables to allow for instantiation Benefits • Adds information/meaning based on other facts/rules • Reduces need for repetition of facts/rules or improves efficiency by reducing code • Facilitates queries • Use of variables allow values to be returned • Any other valid *Any 2 bullets – 1 mark each*	2
5.			• (Provide facilities) for public authorities (e.g. police/MI5/government) to intercept electronic communications • fit equipment to facilitate surveillance (technical services) • pay for systems to assist with interception of electronic communications • pay for the hardware needed to store electronic communication • inform staff of the fact that access to communication data is subject to the RIPA *1 mark for each bullet, maximum 2 marks.*	2
6.	(a)		• Date • Time • Script attached to interface item	1
	(b)		• Recommended items • Name	1
7.			1 mark for correct simple condition found = true/counter = 49 2 marks for correct complex condition found = true OR counter = 49	2

Question			Expected Answer(s)	Max mark
8.			*Any two of the following:* • Allows the client to see/test/feedback on proposed solutions • Subsystems/specific elements can be prioritised and tested as early as possible • A range of proposed solutions can be developed on a small scale instead of the need for full implementation	2
9.			*Any two of the following:* • Frequently accessed data/instructions are held in cache • Faster access memory (on the same chip as processor) • Reducing the need to access slower main memory	2
10.			*Any two of the following:* • End user group/independent test group (1 mark) • Given tasks to perform/observed performing tasks (1 mark) • To provide feedback/evaluate (ease of use/fit for purpose) (1 mark)	2
11.			A primary key with more than one field (or attribute or column).	1

Section 2

Question			Expected Answer(s)	Max mark
12.	(a)		Order no, Item ID	1
	(b)		• Customer to Order + Item to Sale + Order to Sale all related and no others • Two of above three are the correct 1:M • All three above are the correct 1:M *1 mark for each bullet.* *Many representations are possible.*	3
	(c)		Customer.Customer name Customer.Customer address Item.Description Item.Cost Order.Order no (or Sale.Order no) Order.Date Sale.Quantity [Order no]=10728 • Award 1 mark for all four tables (Customer, Item, Order, Sale) • Award 1 mark seven correct fields • Award 1 mark for criteria of [order no] = 10728.	3

Question		Expected Answer(s)	Max mark
	(d)	SUM([Sale.Quantity]*[Item.Cost]) and is placed in the Report Footer • Use of SUM or clear description • Quantity*Item cost used or clear description • Report Footer or Summary field	3
13.	(a)	• Specific processes/instructions/tasks can be allocated to certain processors/core processors (1 mark) • Allowing concurrent/simultaneous execution (of scripts and different media elements) (1 mark)	2
	(b)	Use of RLE • Stores the colour of a pixel and • the number of repetitions of the pixel • Reducing the number of pixel values stored Use of JPEG • Takes shades of colour and stores them as one colour • Which can then be stored as a pixel value and number of repetitions Use of LZW • Uses an algorithm to identify patterns • Assigns each pattern a pointer value • Reducing number of pixel values stored MPEG • Stores (key) frames • (Key) frames saved as JPEG • Delta frames save changes between key frames Any other valid response *Any combination of bullet points stated for a maximum of 3 marks.*	3
	(c)	Create a web based app rather than a native app (1 mark). And any one of the following: This can then be viewed using any browser (regardless of OS) (1 mark). So that there is no need to install an app (on an OS) (1 mark).	2
	(d)	• Encryption is used (to encode the e-mail) • Keys are used to encode or decode data • A public key is used to encrypt/A private key is used to decrypt the data	3
	(e)	• To prevent keylogging • To prevent brute force attacks *Either bullet for 1 mark.*	1

Question			Expected Answer(s)	Max mark
14.	(a)		boolean	1
	(b)		This is one approach to solving this problem. **Reference Language** Line 1. SET valid TO True Line 2. IF Length (mobile_number) <> 11 THEN Line 3. SET valid TO False Line 4. ELSE Line 5. FOR counter FROM 1 TO 11 DO Line 6. IF (Mid(mobile_number, counter, 1) < "0") OR (Mid(mobile_number, counter, 1) > "9") THEN Line 7. SET valid TO False Line 8. END IF Line 9. END FOR Line 10. END IF • 1 mark for checking the length of the string • 1 mark for using a loop to traverse over each character • 1 mark for use of a correct complex if or loop condition (may include check on first character being zero) An additional mark may be awarded for any of the following bullets for a maximum of 2 marks. • 1 mark for use of conditional loop that includes a request for re-entry of mobile number • 1 mark for valid use of a Boolean ○ 1 mark for an error message if an invalid number has been entered	5
	(c)		• Name of a valid parameter AND passed by reference/byRef (1 mark) • As the value will be updated AND returned/passed out (1 mark)	2
	(d)	(i)	A hybrid cloud is a combination of a private and public cloud (1 mark).	1
		(ii)	*Any two of the following:* • Store sensitive data on the private cloud (1 mark) • Can outsource services to public cloud (at times of need) (1 mark) • Can easily expand capacity of public cloud storage without hardware costs (1 mark) • Public cloud use will not result in the purchase of new hardware/servers • Public cloud use reduces cost in relation to backup strategies (1 mark)	2
15.	(a)		• Use an emulator (to imitate the older operating system) • Virtual machine • Compatibility mode	1

Question		Expected Answer(s)	Max mark
(b)		*Any two of the following:* • Different groups/profiles • Different rights/permissions • Set up a public folder	2
(c)	(i)	• Data format conversion/converting camera signals eg serial to parallel. • Buffering/temporary storage of data in transit between the camera and the computer/compensates for differences in speed between the camera and the computer. • Handling of status signals/to ensure camera data is received correctly. • Voltage conversion/to change voltage levels of the camera to relevant levels for the computer. • Protocol conversion/ensure camera and computer adhere to the same protocols. *1 mark for each statement of two different functions – maximum 2 marks.* *Question is a 'state' and so underlined terms on their own are acceptable but any valid description is acceptable.*	2
	(ii)	*Any two of the following:* Bit-Map • Bit mapped graphics can be edited in fine detail at pixel level • More realistic images • Less constrained by mathematical objects Vector • Objects can be layered • Scalable without losing resolution/no pixilation • Editing individual attributes	2
(d)		$90 \times 25 \times 260 \times 200 \times 24$ = 334.7 MB • 1 mark for 1st line – different expressions are acceptable • 1 mark for final answer Fully worked response: $90 \times 25 \times 260 \times 200 \times 24$ = 2,808,000,000 bits = 351,000,000 bytes = 342773.4375 KB = 334.73 MB = 334.7 MB	2
(e)	(i)	Advantage: • Reduces the need for computers/parts to go to landfill • Reduces amount of potentially toxic waste • Any other valid response	1
	(ii)	Advantage: • Newer computers are built to high environmental standards • Use less power/less carbon footprint • Any other valid response	1

Question		Expected Answer(s)	Max mark
16.	(a)	An internal style sheet is embedded within the HTML code for each page (1 mark) whereas an external style sheet is a separate file (that can be used by multiple pages) (1 mark).	2
	(b)	*Any two of the following:* • An external style sheet would be loaded once and (cached locally for future use) (1 mark) • Internal style sheets would be downloaded every time the page is viewed again (1 mark) • Webpages have larger file sizes due to the embedded internal style sheets which take longer to download (1 mark)	2
	(c)	<link rel = "stylesheet" type= "text/css" href= "masterstyle.css">	2
	(d)	H1 {font-family:Tahoma; color:blue; text-align:center} • H1 (or H2) with { } • font-family:Tahoma; • color:blue; • text-align:center *1 mark for each bullet for a maximum of 3 marks.*	3
	(e)	• Make use of a keywords meta tag (to include the terms 'Glasburgh Safari' or 'pandas') (1 mark) • Make use of terms 'Glasburgh Safari' or 'pandas' throughout the body of the pages of the website • Include keywords e.g. ('Glasburgh Safari' or 'pandas') in the title tags (1 mark) • ALT tags on images • Create/submit a sitemap • Any other valid response	2
	(f)	A query could be used to calculate how many tickets are available (1 mark). An appropriate message is generated from the result of the query (code is used to generate a message) (1 mark).	2

Question			Expected Answer(s)	Max mark
17.	(a)	(i)	• Assigns values to (element one of) an array • Assigns values to the Test_mark record *1 mark each, maximum of 2 marks.*	2
		(ii)	89	1
		(iii)	SET average TO (pupil[1].mark_1 + pupil[1].mark_2 + pupil[1].mark_3)/3 • 1 mark for logical average with assignment • 1 mark for reference to the variable pupil at least once	2
	(b)	(i)	2	1
		(ii)	Logic error	1
		(iii)	• Line 3 needs changed • FOR counter FROM 0 TO 3 DO	2
	(c)		A – 74.33 B – 1 C – 57.67	3
	(d)		• Stop/pause program at a defined point • to check the values of the variables (match the expected value)	2

HIGHER COMPUTING SCIENCE 2016

Section 1

Question			Expected Answer(s)	Max mark
1.			• Precision will decrease **(1)** • Range will increase **(1)**	2
2.			95*24 *1280*720*16 = 3·91387939 Gb	2
3.			Concept of inheritance **(1)** Only additional methods and attributes need to be declared for subclasses **(1)**	2
4.			• Rapid Application Development uses minimal planning/reduced analysis • Rapid Application Development involves the creation of prototypes/working software as soon as possible • In Rapid Application Development, the planning and design of a project happens concurrently with the Implementation of the project • Rapid Application Development allows users to feedback during all stages of the development process • Rapid Application Design allows changes to the design to be made at any time throughout the life of the project in response to client feedback	2
5.			• Radio buttons/drop down/restricted choice menu for membership • Calendar for DOB • Member ID automatically generated; use Autonumber for Member ID • Button to submit data	2
6.			• Pupils have read only access to this folder **(1)** • Teachers have read/write access to this folder **(1)**	2
7.	(a)		No single field provides a unique value OR All three fields required to provide a unique value	1
	(b)		• Field/data type • Keys/PK/FK • Validation • Field length/size • Format • Required • Unique • Sample data • Table name	2

Question			Expected Answer(s)	Max mark
8.	(a)		• Head tag isn't closed • H1 tag in head/title • Centre should be center • P1 should be p	2
	(b)	(i)	• To provide a description of the webpage • To provide information to search engine (webcrawlers) • To include key words • To provide information about page creation date/last edit date/author's details etc	1
		(ii)	In the head section	1
9.			Greater demand • for raw materials • transportation of materials • electricity/energy for manufacture and use Disposal • transporting old computers to the dump • poisonous chemicals contained within computer components can contaminate water and air • landfill sites	1

Section 2

Question		Expected Answer(s)	Max mark

10.	(a)	SET total TO 0
		FOR counter FROM 0 TO 5 DO
		  IF SDD[counter] = "B" AND ISDD[counter] = "B" THEN
		    SET total TO total + 1
		  END IF
		END FOR
		SEND ("The total number of pupils attaining a B in both tests was " & total) TO DISPLAY
		
		Visual Studio
		Set total to 0
		For counter = 0 To 5
		  IF SDD[counter] = "B" AND ISDD[counter] = "B" Then
		    lstresults.Items.Add(pupil(counter))
		    total = total + 1
		  End If
		Next
		lstresults.Items.Add("The total number of pupils achieving a B in both tests was")
		lstresults.Items.Add(total)
			5

	(b)	• (Data flow is clearer so) code is more readable/easier to maintain • Portability is improved as code can be reused (without altering variable names) • Aids modularity • Reduces clashes between variable names • Reduces impact or load on main memory • Any other valid response	2

Question			Expected Answer(s)	Max mark
	(c)		• Makes a copy of the array • Increases the number of processing instructions • Increases RAM requirements	2
	(d)		Returns a single value (used in assignment)	1
	(e)	(i)	• Inform employees of access to digital communication • Provide access/encryption keys to authorised authorities/bodies/personnel • Have facilities to store digital communications • Have facilities/software to monitor digital communications	2
		(ii)	Description involving: • Freedom of speech • Privacy	2
11.	(a)		Links to additional pages from Tour Dates, Band Members or Fan pages	1
	(b)		Client-side (scripting)	1
	(c)	(i)	H1 {font-family:Tahoma; color:blue; text-align:center}	3
		(ii)	• One change to the style sheet will change all pages • One style sheet can be applied to multiple pages reducing development time • You can create classes of styles that can then be used on many different HTML elements • Consistent look and feel across multiple web pages • Improve load times because downloaded once • Can be set up for different devices/sizes of screen • Style sheet stored once rather than for multipile pages reducing overall file size	2
	(d)		• The URL should include China Cats or electropop (or both) • The title of each page should include China Cats or electropop (or both) • Meta tags/meta data with appropriate key words e.g. China Cats and electropop • Ensuring there are more links to the site from other sites • Improving the rating given to the site by the search engine crawler • Submit the website to search engines • Keyword loading/stuffing – add more relevant text content to webpages	2
	(e)		Customer knows: • Digital signature/encryption • Site is authenticated e.g. certificate issued by (certification) authority • Site is regulated	2

Question			Expected Answer(s)	Max mark
12.	(a)		• Open source provides support via a community of users/developers • Open source code can be modified/edited • Open source is normally free • Proprietary support is provided by the company who produced it • Proprietary is sometimes free • Emma may already be familiar with the user interface of proprietary software from previous versions Any other valid response	2
	(b)		• Set up a Virtual Machine • This will allow a host operating system to run another operating system	2
	(c)	(i)	• Increasing the number of samples per second • Increasing the number of bits per sample (increasing the range of sounds)	2
		(ii)	• Removes frequencies not heard by humans • Removes the quieter of two simultaneous sounds • Very low frequencies are stored as mono rather than stereo	1
	(d)		• The address bus stores/carries/holds the address of the memory location of the data (currently being accessed/read from) • The data bus transfers data to the processor/register	2
13.	(a)		A=71 B=false C=true D=false	4
	(b)	(i)	• Resets found to false for every non-matching item • Continues looping after target found	1
		(ii)	Remove lines 7 and 8 OR Use a conditional loop until found is true(or end of list)	1
	(c)		• The code for the loop/array values will be present in cache **(1)** • Meaning faster access than going to slower main memory **(1)**	2
14.	(a)		• Real time update of available tickets/e-commerce • Dynamic pages can load user specific content (accept examples) • Ability to create queries/gain feedback or requests for information from users via forms Any other valid response	2

Question			Expected Answer(s)	Max mark

	(b)		• Query/script/search for ticket or weather
			• Criteria:
			  ◦ date 3rd June
			  ◦ log in details e.g. user name and password
			  ◦ geographical location for weather
			  ◦ number of tickets
			• Compare tickets requested with tickets available
			• Returns
			  ◦ the message (if the number of tickets requested is not available)
			  ◦ user's name
			  ◦ current weather which is used to select appropriate weather graphic
				4

	(c)		Customer → Attraction Booking → Attraction → Theme Park 1 mark for each correct relationship	3
	(d)	(i)	Risk of data loss	1
		(ii)	• Increase the frequency of backing up (1) by doing differential/incremental back ups (1) • Make differential backup (1) saving changes since last full backup (1) • Make incremental backups (1) saving changes since last backup of any type (1)	2
	(e)		The Data Protection Act **(1)** makes it an offence to share data without the data subjects consent **(1)**	2
15.	(a)		DECLARE athletes[7] As athleteData	2
	(b)		DECLARE athletes[] INITIALLY athleteData ("Salma", "Hussain", 324, True, 45.12, 67·5) OR SET athletes[] TO athleteData ("Salma", "Hussain", 324, True, 45.12, 67·5) OR athletes().forename = "Salma" athletes().surname = "Hussain" athletes().runnerNumber = 324 athletes().professional = True athletes().seasonBest = 45.12 athletes().weight = 67.5	3
	(c)		Line 1 SET minimum TO athletes[0].seasonBest Line 2 FOR counter FROM 1 TO 7 DO Line 3 IF athletes[counter].seasonBest < minimum THEN Line 4 minimum = athletes[counter].seasonBest Line 5 END IF Line 6 END FOR	5
	(d)	(i)	To create a file called "winner" inside the folder MyAthletes on the C drive	1
		(ii)	To write the fastest time to the file called winner.txt	1

Question	Expected Answer(s)	Max mark
(e)	1st mark for naming a technique: • Dry Run • Breakpoint 2nd mark for related description **Dry Run** Manual run through of code often involving a pen and paper to try to identify errors **Breakpoint** Stop the program **OR** Inspect the value of variables	2

HIGHER COMPUTING SCIENCE 2017

Section 1

Question			Expected Answer(s)	Max mark
1.			$-32{,}768$ to $+32{,}767$ OR -2^{16-1} to $(2^{16-1}) - 1$	2
2.			• Requirements elicitation e.g. ○ Interview Client ○ Inspect documentation ○ Observation • Produce(software) specification • Identify inputs/processes/outputs • Identify scope/boundaries • Functional requirements detailing features of software	2
3.			$96000 \times 16 \times 120 \times 2$ $= 368\,640\,000/8$ $= 46\,080\,000/1024$ $= 45\,000/1024$ $= 43 \cdot 9$ Mb	3
4.			A compound key is a key field made up of two or more fields (that are primary keys in other tables/foreign keys) A surrogate key is created to introduce a primary key (in the absence of a natural primary key)	2
5.			Unauthorised access to personal data (sent to third parties through the tracking cookie)	1
6.			• A public key is used to encrypt the personal data • A private key is used to decrypt the personal data	2
7.	(a)		• High resolution displays • High-contrast themes • Icons supplemented with auditory feedback • Screen magnifying software • Screen reader software • Speech recognition software • Braille display/keyboard • Appropriate colour schemes	1
	(b)		• Subtitles/closed caption/text transcript • Replace system sounds like beeps with visual notifications and captioned text • Use visual warnings, such as a blinking title bar or a flashing border, whenever the computer generates a sound • (Noise cancelling) headphones	1

Question			Expected Answer(s)	Max mark
8.			• Uses classes/sub-classes • Classes are created with attributes and methods • Subclasses inherit code of a superclass • Objects of these classes can be instantiated • Methods perform an operation • Attributes store properties/values (for an instance) • Subclasses need only define additional attributes and methods	2
9.	(a)		RECORD BookDetails IS {STRING title, STRING author, INTEGER number of pages, REAL price}	2
	(b)		Create variable ListOfBooks [999] of (data type) BookDetails OR DECLARE ListOfBooks AS ARRAY OF BookDetails INITIALLY [] * 999	2

Section 2

Question			Expected Answer(s)	Max mark

10.	(a)		SET minpos TO 0
			SET minimum TO temps(0)
			FOR index FROM 1 TO 23 DO
			IF temps (index) < minimum THEN
			    SET minpos TO index
			    SET minimum TO temps (index)
			END IF
			NEXT index
			SEND " The... was" & minimum & "Celsius..." at hour" & index
			OPEN "low.txt"
			SEND minimum TO FILE
			Close "low.txt"
			
			SET minpos TO 0
			FOR index FROM 1 TO 23 DO
			IF temps (index) < temps(minpos) THEN
			    SET minpos TO index
			END IF
			NEXT index
			SEND " The... was" & temps(minpos) & "Celsius..." at hour" & minpos
			OPEN "low.txt"
			SEND temps(minpos) TO FILE
			Close "low.txt"
				7

Question			Expected Answer(s)	Max mark

	(b)		• File management:
			  ◦ identifies a free space on backing storage to place file
			  OR
			  ◦ Updates/checks file directory
			• Memory management:
			  ◦ locates data in main memory
			  OR
			  ◦ allocates main memory for process
			• Input/Output:
			  ◦ transfer from memory to backing storage
			• Resource allocation:
			  ◦ managing processes and memory
				2

	(c)	(i)	(see table below)	2

Iteration	Total	Average
2	18	9
3	30	10

Question			Expected Answer(s)	Max mark
		(ii)	Calculation results in the wrong data type i.e. real for the variable average Make average a real variable	2
	(d)		• Change the number 23 to END OF LIST • Use a conditional loop that utilises END OF LIST/FILE as a condition • Use a function to determine the size of the array • Accept a parameter that is used to define the size of the array	1
	(e)		• Remote access to control heating when not at home • Use of geolocation can automatically turn heating off when no one is home • Takes account of external weather forecast and adjusts temperature accordingly • Real time temperature monitoring through mobile devices can reduce unnecessary gas/fuel use • Data can be analysed to determine how quickly a home heats and how slowly it loses heat meaning that the boiler can be used more efficiently • Multi room control systems prevent rooms being overheated when not in use	2
11.	(a)		Customer ← Booking ← Driver ← Car	3
	(b)	(i)	Customer.Known As Booking.Booking ID Booking.From Booking.To Booking.Cost Car.Registration OR Driver.Registration	3
		(ii)	(Booking.)Booking ID=12345	1
	(c)		• The onmouseover event is triggered • executing the mouseOver function • changing the (style) colour to yellow(of the phrase "Welcome to Super Taxi"/heading)	2

Question		Expected Answer(s)	Max mark
	(d)	<meta name="keywords" content="super,taxi,.....">	2

	(e)	Search (index) for key words in
		  ◦ title tags
		  ◦ alt tags
		  ◦ body/page/content
		  ◦ URL
		• Checking links to the site from other sites
		• Data analytics e.g. hit rate, location by proximity, filters, prominent social media presence
		• Algorithms to determine relevance
			2

	(f)	Head section of the HTML	1
	(g)	• External more efficient as loaded once/cached but used by several pages • Internal loaded every time a page is accessed	2
12.	(a)	• Arrival OR • departure Any one bullet from: • A formal parameter can be a copy of the actual parameter • A formal parameter can be a pointer/placeholder to the actual parameter • A formal parameter can control the flow of data e.g. by reference or by value	2
	(b)	The values are switched/passed into the incorrect parameters 10 – 13 results in –3 hours_parked is less than 1	2
	(c)	Watchpoints are used to stop execution when the value of a specific variable changes/pre-determined conditions are met This allows the programmer to compare the value with the expected value	2
	(d)	• More efficient as memory assigned to a local variable becomes available once function is terminated • Allows variables of the same name in different modules without affecting others • Aids modularity	2
13.	(a)	• Users given task/scenario to perform on the software • Suitable target set of users e.g. novice, experienced • Observation of performance of users • Feedback is given to developers	2
	(b)	• Sort by • Your basket • Page styles/(Gallery/List View) • Buttons: Buy; Pre Order; View Selection; View All • "i" icon (next to pre-order)	1

Question		Expected Answer(s)	Max mark
	(c)	• Connection with server/database established OR reference to PHP/server-side scripting • Data captured on webpage form is used to construct a query • A query is used to check number of available items and release date • The result of the query is processed/returned (to update the webpage)	3
	(d) (i)	Description of backup with frequency e.g. • Back up all data/(full back up) weekly/daily • Save changes since last full backup (differential) daily/hourly • Saving changes since last back up of any type (incremental) daily/hourly Backup type name and frequency	2
	(ii)	Cloud Offline Off-site repository Distributed storage Mirror disk Full/incremental/differential (not mentioned in part (i))	1
	(e)	• All text in correct colours: "Welcome To" and "Glasgow" would be displayed in red; "PC Bits" in blue • Alignment & size: all text centred, PC Bits double size/200%	2

Welcome To

PCBits

Glasgow

Question		Expected Answer(s)	Max mark
14.	(a)	• Public cloud does not mean open access • Password protected space is rented to public • Data may be encrypted • Data protected by firewall	2
	(b) (i)	Vector as: • You can drag individual objects without affecting others • Ear could be grouped as a set of objects • Objects can be layered • Attributes/co-ordinates of ears can be changed	2
	(ii)	• Vector increases • Bitmap stays the same	2
15.	(a)	• Address of instruction placed on address bus • Read line (on control bus) is activated • Contents of location (instruction) transferred to a register along data bus • Instruction decoded/executed	3

Question			Expected Answer(s)	Max mark
(b)	(i)		• Stores frequently accessed instructions/data • Faster access times than main memory • Fewer accesses to slower main memory • On the same chip as the processor • Cache is static RAM (faster)	2
	(ii)		• Instructions 2/3 will already be (pre-loaded) in cache i.e. a cache hit will occur • Data in location 2000 will already be in cache improving access time/instruction time.	2
(c)			16777216 colours is better than 65536	2
(d)	(i)		• Interframe saves the differences between frames • Intraframe compresses a single frame (using RLE or 'blocking' shades of colours)	2
	(ii)		• More effective compression for a singer performer • (Differential/delta/i/p) Interframes will be smaller for a performance with fewer movements • (Differential/delta/i/p) Interframes will be larger for performance with more movement • More key/delta frames will be needed as dancers will be moving around	2

Acknowledgements

Permission has been sought from all relevant copyright holders and Hodder Gibson is grateful for the use of the following:

GooDween123/Shutterstock.com (2015 Section 2 page 10).